Prayers for Daughters

© 2010 by Barbour Publishing, Inc.

Written and compiled by Debora M. Coty.

ISBN 978-1-60260-746-0

Published by Barbour Publishing, Inc., P.O. Box 719, Uhrichsville, Ohio 44683, www.barbourbooks.com

Our mission is to publish and distribute inspirational products offering exceptional value and biblical encouragement to the masses.

Member of the
Evangelical Christian
Publishers Association

Printed in China.

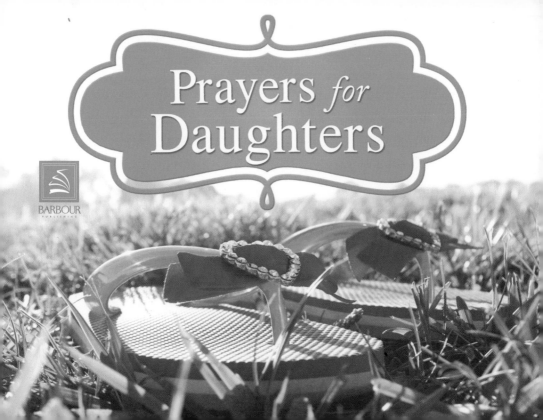

Prayers *for* Daughters

BARBOUR
PUBLISHING

Abba Father, my beloved Papa God, teach me the crucial difference between knowing about You. . . and knowing You. It's head versus heart, isn't it? Like the difference between knowing all about love and being in love.

Help me remember, Lord God Almighty, that You always hear me when I call Your holy name. Even a simple "O, my God!" is an IM (instant message) directly to You. Teach me to respect and use Your name wisely.

Thank You for making me a princess,
a daughter of the King. Help me act and
think like a princess. Amen.

You'll miss 100% of the shots you never take.

A POSTER ON THE BEDROOM
DOOR OF A DAUGHTER

Dear God, thank You for the special gifts You've given just to me—my heart, my mind, my unique talents and abilities. Like Christmas gifts, I want to open and enjoy them, not stuff them in my closet or under my bed to be ignored and forgotten.

I'm so glad You think I'm beautiful, Father.
I'm an original by the top Designer of all time!
You use only quality materials, and Your
fashions are always in style!

Jesus, pour Yourself inside of me,
toes to hairline. I choose today to be filled
with You rather than to be filled with me.

Everlasting God, You sent just enough manna to the Israelites when they needed it; not too much, not too little, but just enough for the day ahead. Thank You for sending me just the right amount of help at the exact time I need it. Not before, not after, but right on time.

Faith is a verb. . .an action. Help me believe
and move forward, always forward.

Lord, like I sometimes crave food, I want to crave You, to want nothing more than to fill my empty space inside with You. Teach me to hunger and thirst after righteousness and not to settle for hamburger when I can have steak!

My Strong Rock, thank You for measuring success by faithfulness, not results. Teach me that my part is to faithfully listen to You and obey. Your part is to take care of the results.

Whatever your hand finds to do,
do it with all your might.
ECCLESIASTES 9:10 NASB

Today, I promise to speak the truth in love (Proverbs 12:18) and think before I speak. Is what's about to come out of my mouth:

T = TRUTHFUL?
H = HELPFUL?
I = INSPIRING?
N = NECESSARY?
K = KIND?

Cleansers, foundation, mascara, lip gloss. . .kindness, patience, gentleness, self-control. Lord, help me to focus as much on my inner beauty as my outer beauty.

Papa God, I'm sorry for the wrong things I do and say and think. Thank You for taking the awful weight off my shoulders by forgiving my sins. Remind me that I don't have to lug around guilt like an overstuffed backpack.

DEFINITION OF SIN:

STATIC THAT DROPS YOUR GOD-CALLS.

Help me appreciate my family, gracious Father, for they are Your way of helping me begin to understand Your unconditional love. Amen.

Lord, I'm so grateful that You heal us when we're brokenhearted (Psalm 147:3). Your supernatural Band-Aids put all the pieces of my broken heart back together!

You told me to practice faith in my own family (1 Timothy 5:4). Okay, Father, but if it's anything like the piano, I may have to practice for a l-o-o-o-n-g time before I get it right.

THANK YOU, EVER-FORGIVING SAVIOR, THAT
WHEN I'M DIRTY WITH SIN, I CAN COME TO YOU FOR
FORGIVENESS AND YOU WILL CLEAN ME UP AS SPOTLESS
AND FRESH AND PURE AS NEW-FALLEN SNOW.

Father, help me to realize that my kindness toward others is like opening the blinds to Your glorious Sonshine. Some people may never see Jesus except through me. Amen.

I choose to love God, not for what He does or doesn't do, but for who He is.

Jesus, make me like a new puppy. Teach me to respect the doors You place in my life for my own good, to walk through the doors You open, and to not dig and claw and howl at the doors closed by Your loving hand.

Help me remember that the Bible isn't a list of do's and don't's, but love letters from You, my heavenly Father, to me, Your daughter. I love You with all my heart and cherish Your sweet words.

Prayer is the nerve that makes the
muscles move in the hand of God.

Some people say I look like my mother. It makes sense, for I am her child. I'm Your child, too, Father God. Help me to imitate You, to follow Your example, and to look and sound more like You every day. Amen.

ou said Your children are the salt and light of the world (Matthew 5:13-14), much needed to add flavor to blandness and lead the way through the dark. Help me, Lord, to pass the salt and hold my candle high for those in my neighborhood and social circles.

Be strong and let your heart take courage,
all you who hope in the LORD.
PSALM 31:24 NASB

Teach us about Your incredible nature through Your Hebrew names, Lord. You are Jehovah Jirah (our Provider). You know of our needs, even before we ask. Thank You for Your gracious provision.

Jehovah Rophe (our Healer), You see our deep wounds inside,
where no one else can. Please touch and heal
our brokenness with Your tender mercies. Amen.

Sheep aren't too bright, are they? They follow each other right off cliffs and into major trouble because of poor choices. Lead me, Jehovah Rohi (our Shepherd), to make good choices that will glorify You.

Like the American flag that flew over Fort McHenry during the War of 1812 and inspired our national anthem, "The Star-Spangled Banner," You, Jehovah Nissi (our Victorious Banner), are the flag that flies over me. You are my King and I belong to the kingdom of heaven, now and for all time to come.

Jehovah Shalom (our Peace), when the world feels upside down, when everything falls apart and confusion clouds my brain, fill my heart with Your supernatural peace. . .the peace that passes all understanding and keeps our hearts and minds in Christ Jesus (Philippians 4:7).

Life isn't always fair, but God is always God.

Jesus, when I'm fighting a strong temptation, help me remember it's more effective to refocus my attention than trying to resist the temptation. Like when I'm tempted to spill the secret a friend confided in me, if I focus on praying for her instead, I'm able to resist the urge.

Lord, I'm so glad You love me for me.
Sometimes I just don't feel smart or pretty or good at
anything. Thank You that whether I feel lovable or not,
You love me not for what I do, but for the me You created.

So hey, whatever, Lord. Do I mean it?
Sure I do. Whatever You want me to be, I'll be.
Whatever You want me to do, I'll do. I may not always
understand why, or even like the final decision,
but I trust You enough for "whatever."

I'm so glad You didn't make me a Barbie, Lord. I would dislike having to be perfect all the time—perfect hair, trendy clothes, impeccable makeup, spike heels on my little plastic feet. Thanks for messiness, crazy hair, and torn jeans!

Fill me today, Jesus, with Your light and love.

Preach the Gospel at all times
and when necessary use words.

ST. FRANCIS OF ASSISI

If I was a designer purse, I know what the price tag would say: "Paid in full by the blood of Jesus." Wow! To think I'm worth so much to You, that You'd pay for me with the life of Your only Son. Thank You, Father!

You told Joshua to conquer a city by yelling at a wall. You told Noah to build a boat in a desert. You told Peter he'd catch fish on the other side of the boat (duh, there's no wall underwater; don't fish swim on both sides of a boat?). Each crazy instruction was the beginning of a miracle. Help me obey Your still, small voice, Lord, even when it doesn't seem to make sense.

You didn't say we have to WIN, You just want us to cross the finish line (Philippians 3:14 and 2 Timothy 4:7). Thank You for providing strength and perseverance when we think we can't go on.

*When I am afraid, I will
trust in you.*
PSALM 56:3 NIV

Like zacchaeus in Luke 19, I want
to make You Lord of my stuff, Jesus.

I know that You're not just the God of huge, earth-shaking miracles, but You're also the God of little, everyday miracles in my life. So cool!

Father, I pray that today You'll be able to measure my love for You by how willing I am to tell others about You. Amen.

In order to truly know the Lord Most High,
we must become the servants most low.

I'm a real live daughter of the King, not a statue.
Make my ears hear cries for help, my eyes see
the needs of others, and my hands serve as my
heavenly Father's hands here on earth.

Lord, sometimes it's hard to be in the middle. . .not still a child, but not grown up yet either. It's comforting to know I will always be Your little girl, no matter how old I am, and You'll welcome me to climb up in Your lap for a cuddle anytime.

Help me remember that You've called me to live a
holy life — a life *set* apart. A life that reflects Jesus.
I don't want to be a cheap copy of someone else.
I want to be an original.

Lord, when my thoughts start scraping bottom like slimy pond scum, help me switch brain channels to that which is true, pure, and lovely (Philippians 4:8). In other words, I want to tune into my internal MTV (Master's Terrific Viewpoint) program. Now that's a reality show!

Keep reminding me, Father, that there's no such thing as a little white lie. Untruths are all the same color—midnight black—and weigh exactly the same on Your scale: a ton.

Father of mercy and God of all comfort,
I want to be as faithful to You as I am
to my favorite pair of jeans. Amen.

Just like I wouldn't dream of going 24 hours without hearing from my best friend, help me commit to reading Your Word every single day. After all, the Bible is like text messages from my supernatural best friend.

God reveals Himself only to those with humble
hearts. . .never to the proud. Why should He?
Pride blares like an out-of-control iPod
and drowns out the voice of God.

Giver of all good things, I don't mean to treat You as my personal Santa Claus in the sky. Help me spend just as much time thanking You and praising You as I do asking for things on my wish list.

Kindness begins with the eyes.
Like the Good Samaritan, help me, Lord, to see the
needs of others today. And then act in kindness.

Father God, I don't want to be so caught up in busyness that my focus shifts to what seems important at the moment, rather than what actually is. Please don't let hurry kill kindness in my life today.

"All things are possible with God."

Mark 10:27 NASB

Help me plan to spend time today with those who love You as much as I do. Encourage my faith, Papa God, through the company I keep.

Jesus, don't let me get so busy doing things for You that I forget my number one goal is to become like You. Amen.

Help me explain to those who don't know You that we don't ooze into Your family by being good. Nobody would make it if we did! We must deliberately choose adoption by faith. It's s-o-o-o wonderful to be Your daughter!

Father, You said being part of the body of believers is Your plan for me. Okay. I'll be a hand to serve meals to the homeless, or a heart to pray for the sick, or a mouth to teach little kids about Jesus, or even a foot that carries trash from a neighbor's yard if You want me to.

He Who my soul loves, Your Word says to flee from evil desires of youth (2 Timothy 2:22). Give my feet Wings to run away from any magazine, website, TV show, movie, CD, or person who tempts me to do or think wrong things.

In order to train myself to be godly (1 Timothy 4:7), help me develop good habits that radiate Your presence and to drop ugly habits that are all about me. Amen.

Thank You for being my power source!
Plug me in and watch me go!

Some people may never see God's love if
they don't see it through me.
Today, I want to radiate Your love, Father.

Lord, You said to pray for those who are mean to us (Matthew 5:44). It's funny how when I pray for the girl who treats me badly, somehow I start to feel differently toward her. Something changes inside me. Could it be that You use my prayers for others to actually help me?

My mom treasures her pearl necklace because it belonged to Grandma. In the same way, I'm thankful that You consider me a "pearl of great price" who is valuable beyond measure (Matthew 13:45-46). Wow! To think that You treasure me!

Thank You, Father, for being involved in every
detail of my life. Not just the big ones,
but the tiny ones, too. You truly care about my
toenails, earlobes, freckles, and all.

God makes a home for the lonely (Psalm 68:6).
We never again need to feel alone or unloved.
There's always a warm hug, a cold glass of milk, and
cookies baking in God's kitchen when we get home.

I'm so glad that I can trust You with all the secrets of my heart, Jesus. You always listen. And You always understand.

Thank You for being You. The Great I Am.
The same yesterday, today, and tomorrow.
I want to shout from the rooftops:
My God is an AWESOME God!

Lord, make me as wise as an owl, gentle as a bunny, alert as a cat, stubborn as a donkey (about my faith!), strong as a horse, and loyal as a watchdog.

Now faith is being sure of what we hope for and certain of what we do not see.

When life doesn't seem fair, and the good guys finish last, help me remember that in the end, things will flip-flop: the first shall be last and the last shall be first (Matthew 20:16).

During sad times, help me remember to cry a river, but laugh a rainbow. It's okay to mourn our losses, but just like Your rainbow was a symbol of hope to Noah after the flood, we have hope that tomorrow will be better. Our tears will dry and we will laugh again.

When my brain is fried, my feet ache, my arms are tired,
or my soul is just plain weary, thank You,
Father, that in You I can find rest. Amen.

Like the sand castle at the beach that's washed away by incoming waves, help me remember that beliefs built on the shifting sand of man-made religions will never last. But faith built on the solid rock of Jesus, now that's permanent!

You didn't create us all to be brilliant or famous or Olympic athletes. We're all so different, but everyone is special to You. Help me respect and appreciate our differences.

Why is it, Jesus, that when others hurt me, I want to hurt them back? You never paid back evil for evil, and I know You don't want me to, either. Please help me rise above seeking revenge and leave justice up to You. Amen.

When I'm in trouble, whom do I turn to? When I need help, whom do I call? You, my Rescuer and Savior, are my very real help in times of trouble. Thank You for being my own personal EMS: Everyday Miracle Service.

Prayer is the least and the most we can do.

Help me care more about others, Jesus.
Remind me that as I treat with compassion those
who are hungry, thirsty, lonely, poor, or sick, I'm really
treating You with that same compassion.

Thank You, Jesus, for being my example of obedience, even when it's hard. You were born to suffer terribly and die on a cross for the sins of the very people who killed You. You never complained or ran away because You knew it was Your Father's will and how very much He loved you. Make me obedient like You.

Thank You, my Creator, for knowing every
little part of me inside and out...
and for loving me anyway.

Help me to love others because You first loved me.
I want to love them consistently, steadily, thoroughly. . .
just the way You love me.

Filter my vision with love, Papa God.
Help me see only the best in others.
I want to have my Father's eyes.

Lord, teach me the difference between bringing Your light to those who live in the darkness. . .and setting up my own bedroom there in the cave.

Restorer of my soul, make me always feel the sunburn of sin, and not get so tanned by bad habits that I no longer feel the sting of conviction. Amen.

Don't let anyone put you down because you're young.
Teach believers with your life: by word,
by demeanor, by love, by faith, by integrity.
1 TIMOTHY 4:12 MSG

What a relief to know You've already won the battle over death
for those who believe! Talk about extreme contests!
Jesus conquered the grave so death is no longer frightening.
Help me remember that the worst thing that could happen to me
is that I'll wake up in heaven with Jesus—how exciting!

I'm so happy that nothing happens by accident.
You are LARGE and in charge!

We only have seven days in a week. Help me to use each one, Lord, to make a difference.

Oops! I rolled my eyes again when Mom called me to clean up my room. I wasn't going to do that. . .but I forgot. Thanks, Jesus, that You never forget, and You never roll your eyes when I call on You.

Help me lock the door of my lips and
not let any nasty words escape.

Jesus, I am so grateful that You are my friend—
my best friend Who sticks closer than a brother.
You stay by my side, protect me, and always
want what's best for me. Thanks!

Make me more aware of all the people around me who are hurting or sick. Some are sick inside where it doesn't show. You are the Great Healer, and so many are in need of Your healing touch. I want to lift them up in prayer.

Papa God, thank You so much for allowing me to belong.
I belong to You and You belong to me.
Forever and always. Amen.

Make me a mirror today. When others look at me,
I want them to see Jesus reflected in my life.

Sometimes life is so confusing. Thank You, all-knowing Father, that we don't have to understand everything You're doing in our lives. You ask us only to trust You.

Jesus came to bring the touch of God to humanity. . . and the touch of humanity to God. He came to the earth as Creator in created form. He loves us that much.

Help me remember, Lord, that to change my behavior,
I first have to change my thinking.
The way I act starts with what's happenin' in my
head. No stinkin' thinkin' for me!

Father God, give me courage to get close to people. The risk of rejection is scary sometimes, but like the first two travelers in the story of the Good Samaritan, it's way too easy to not give help to someone when you're avoiding them on the other side of the road. Distance may feel safe, but it's the wimpy way out.

thanks for the living water You provide when we're wiped out. I don't want to settle for a trickle when You want to give me Niagara Falls!

Lord, send me a prayer partner. I want a close girlfriend to pray with as well as for. How awesome to know someone is praying especially for me!

Pray all the time; thank God no matter what happens. This is the way God wants you who belong to Christ Jesus to live.

1 Thessalonians 5:17–18 MSG

In these days of instant everything—instant soup, instant mac and cheese, instant messaging— give me patience to wait on You to act in Your own perfect timing, Lord.

Fraidy cat, fraidy cat, run away home. Sigh. I get so tired of being scared, Lord. Scared of being laughed at, rejected, criticized, or even ignored. Strengthen me with Your courage and help me speak up for what's right. Amen.

Sometimes no one understands me. I feel like an orphan.
Thank You for being a Father to the fatherless,
my Papa God. You always get me.

There are so many people who have so little, Lord, and You have given me so much. Help me to reach out to help others. Even if I don't have extra money to give, I have arms and legs that can do.

†hank You, Father, for the amazing privilege of becoming Your daughter through Your saving power.

Salvation is found in no one else.
ACTS 4:12 NIV

Teach me, Lord, that holiness is not just for my mom or Sunday school teacher or even those preachers on TV. Holiness is about getting to know You better. Holiness is what You want from me.

I never ever want to allow the love and pursuit of things to lead me away from my faith, Father. Things bought with money will just burn one day. Help me focus on what will last. Amen.

Help me show by my actions that what's
important to You is important to me.

Speaker of truth, make me more aware of the destructiveness of gossip. Talking about people is like shredding a fine piece of art with a butcher knife. You created each of us as a masterpiece. I want to honor You by respecting them.

When I'm drained, remind me to recharge my batteries in the powerful presence of You, God!

Bring more Christian friends into my life, heavenly Father.
I know that the people I hang with have a huge influence on me.
Like they say, if you hang out with dogs,
you're gonna get fleas!

I take great care in selecting just the right lip gloss. Help me to be just as careful, Lord, of the words that come from my lips. It would be better if I grabbed a glue stick by mistake and sealed my lips shut than to allow ugly speech to spill out and pollute the air around me.

King of glory, make me realize that I live an inside-out life. What's on the inside shows on the outside! If I fill my head and heart with trash, I'll eventually become trashy. It's like wearing filthy, holey underwear on top of my clothes!

As God's children, we're heirs of an amazing inheritance! S-o-o-o much better than Aunt Myrtle's silver tea service, or Grandpa's coin collection, eternal life in heaven is our awesome dowry. And it's out of this world!

God is more concerned about changes of the heart than information download. He doesn't care how much we know, but He knows how much we care.

I can do everything through Christ,
who gives me strength.
PHILIPPIANS 4:13 NLT

Lord, help me remember that envy and jealousy are hideous in Your sight, but tenderness is beyond beautiful. You love it when I'm tender in surrender. Please tenderize my heart.

Prayers are verbal faith. Generosity is faith
with legs. Father, increase my faith. Amen.

Giver of courage, continuously remind me that perfect love ejects all fear (1 John 4:18). Whether it's fear of rejection, being alone, pain, death, failure, or even success, fear cannot hang out in the presence of love. You, God, are perfect love.

Lord, let me not be so delighted about the ugly zit on the face of my tormentor that I ignore the pimple on my own. Help me focus on fixing my own faults before I zero in on those of others.

Thank You, Master Creator, for putting me together in my mother's womb just exactly the way You wanted me. I am truly fearfully and wonderfully made (Psalm 139:14)!

I'm so glad that You are my help in times of trouble (Psalm 46:1). You're always on duty. You never sleep. You never sneeze. You're never distracted. You never go away on vacation. Thank You for always answering my calls for help.

Prayer isn't just a one-time event in our crazy-busy day; it's in every thankful breath that we take throughout the day.

Sometimes I wish You would send a paper airplane down from heaven with a message written on it, Lord. Or send me a celestial CD. Or text me. But instead You speak to my heart with Your still, small voice. Help me to be quiet and listen for Your whisper so I don't miss it.

Send me a chill pill, God who calmed the stormy seas, When a problem seems unfixable. Please remind me that everyday miracles are Your thing. It's what You do.

Help me remember, Lord, that the devil attacks us with temptation at our weakest moments, when our defenses are down and we are most vulnerable. Give me Your armor to protect myself: the shield of faith, the sword of the Spirit, and the breastplate of righteousness.

Father, I know You rejoice when I speak out about what is right (Proverbs 23:16). Give me courage when I'm afraid to open my mouth. And let me feel You rejoicing! Amen.

One of the promises You made in the Bible is that if children obey their parents, "it will go well with you" (Ephesians 6:1–3). You also said it pleases You when we're obedient (Colossians 3:20). Help me remember, Lord, when I feel like I have better things to do than listen to Mom or Dad, that obedience doesn't require feeling like it. Just doing it.

You made ninety-year-old Sarah a mother. You made a prostitute, Rahab, an honored ancestor of Jesus. You morphed a lonely little Jewish orphan into gorgeous Queen Esther. You can make anyone into anything. Thank You, Father, for the construction You're doing on me!

Jesus, when I feel like a loser, or dumb, or afraid to try something new, help me remember that when I'm weak, then I'm strong (2 Corinthians 12:10). No human can do everything. But You can. You're the original Superman. When I depend on Your strength, it's like I have superpowers.

When things don't make sense, when good goes underground and bad guys get rewarded, remind me that the secret things belong to You (Deuteronomy 29:29). The secret things—the things we don't understand—belong to You. They're Yours. You own them and are always in control.

A joyful heart makes a cheerful face.
PROVERBS 15:13 NASB

Master of heaven and mirth, I'm so glad You
have a sense of humor and love for me to laugh!
You created goofy aardvarks, silly spoonbill platypuses,
penguins in their little tuxes. . .and me!

When the software of my soul is corrupted with sin,
thank You for deleting the file and rebooting me.
Ah, the relief of starting fresh!

Lord, help me remember that patience is really a verb; it's something we do. Help me show Your love through my patience today. Amen.

Sometimes Satan, the master of deceit,
masquerades lies as truth. I get confused,
unsure of the real truth. Show me the truth,
Your truth, Lord, through Your Word.

You said that whatever I do or say, I should do it in Your name (Colossians 3:17). So I'm putting Your label on everything I create or touch or even say. Whoa! No cheap imitations; I want to put Your label only on the very best.

Joy is such an amazing thing, Lord. It's not the same as happiness, is it? Joy isn't dependent on our circumstances, so we can be joyful even when bad things happen. You said the joy of the Lord is our strength (Nehemiah 8:10); fill me with Your joy—and strength—today!

✝hank You God, that You're able to do exceeding abundantly beyond all that I ask or think (Ephesians 3:20). Wow! I can hardly imagine the wonderful things You have in store for me—even beyond my wildest dreams!

I want to hang out with those who build my faith,
not go bungee jumping with the devil.

Doesn't Your Word say to loathe my neighbor? You know, when she snubs me or talks about me behind my back? No? Oh, it says to love my neighbor. I'm glad You're the maker of miracles, because sometimes I need one, Lord.

Teach me, heavenly Father, that prayer
is more for me to understand what You
want than for me to get what I want.

When I worry about the future, remind me that You already know the plans You have for me; plans for my best good; plans that give me fantastic hope for the future (Jeremiah 29:11). Amen.

Father, the Bible says that we shouldn't think we're all that. That we should humbly put ourselves last. Then when the time is right, when we need it most, You will honor us by moving us to the front of the line (1 Peter 5:6).

The more I'm aware of what Christ has done for me, the less critical and judgmental I am toward others. Thank You, Jesus, for dying on the cross in my place.

You said that where my treasure is, there will my heart be also (Matthew 6:21). But what's in my treasure chest, Lord? It's what I think about most, isn't it? That's the treasure that captures my heart. Help me make my treasure the golden kind that will last forever, not the weak and temporary kind that will crumple like aluminum foil.

Thanks for wanting more than anything to hear from me through Twitter prayers, Father—little snippet prayers that I can shoot off to You any time during the day or night. That way we keep in constant communication like the BFFs we really are.

God assured us, "I'll never let you down,
never walk off and leave you."
HEBREWS 13:5 MSG

When my feelings are hurt by an inconsiderate act or thoughtless comment, help me remember that a joyful heart is good medicine (Proverbs 17:22). Laughter is healing! Like a vitamin shot for the heart!

You, Most Excellent One, are greater than the greatest sale at the mall! You're bigger than the Empire State Building! You're wider than the Pacific Ocean! You're higher than Mt. Everest. No one can grasp how enormous You are. Yet You love little me. Thank You!

I don't want to be a spiritual wimp.
Make me a spiritual ninja, Lord, equipped with the
unbeatable weapon of Your Word, which is sharper
than any two-edged blade. Amen.

Help me remember that all my talents and abilities come from You. I'm merely the rosebud; You are the Master Gardener. It's only because of Your water, fertilizer, and loving care that I bloom and grow.

Ever-laughing God, Creator of giggles and glee,
You tickle my funny bone and my soul. Open my eyes to
the humor all around me that releases joy—Your joy—
inside me. Bubble me over with Jesus-joy!

God of the whole earth, fill me with dreams.
Big dreams. Your dreams for me. Amen.

Remind me daily, Lord, that holiness is an act of the will. I choose whether to honor You with my behavior, with my life. . .or not.

Loving Father of prodigals and runaways, thank You
that no matter how far from home I stray,
You always love me unconditionally and welcome
me back with arms open wide.

Lord, I pray for the men and women who are away from their homes and families fighting for our country. Please bless each of them as they sacrifice their comfort and peace so that I might have freedom and safety.
Amen.

My strength and my song, help me learn Your precious Word. I want to memorize scripture so that I can tuck it away in my heart. That way, even if there's no Bible around, You can speak to me every time and in any place I need to hear from You.

Jesus, when I'm lonely, thank You for being there. It warms my heart when You're always happy to see me.

Creator of patience, please give me more. When I get frustrated, help me adjust my goals and expectations of others. Remind me that it's me who has the problem, not them. You're patient with me every day of my life; I want to extend that patience to others.

Thank You, Jesus, for making a difference
in my life that is evident to my friends,
especially those who know me best.

Father of mankind, help me remember that You love all Your children equally. Even though someone may look or act differently than me, You love them just as much as You love me. Not better, not worse, but with equal passion.

We're all Your favorites!

Son of the Most High, bless our country and guide our leaders. We were founded on principles that honor You; please turn our nation's focus back to biblical truths. Amen.

Fire tests the purity of silver and gold,
but a person is tested by being praised.

PROVERBS 27:21 NLT

The Bible says You don't want Your children to just squeak by. You want us to have a full, overflowing, abundant life in Christ. Enrich my life with Your Spirit, Lord!

I'm so in awe of Your power, Creator of heaven and earth. You spoke the world into existence. The stars bounced into place in the midnight sky and the sun rose from nowhere at Your command. You created the air that we breathe and the lungs that draw it in. Thank You for life!

Doing right is a big deal. Forgiveness when I botch it up is an even bigger deal. I'm so glad Your tote bag of forgiveness is bottomless.

I know the Golden Rule, Father: Do unto others as I would want them to do unto me. That means being kind and considerate. But instead I sometimes turn that around backwards and don't do unto others because they don't do unto me. Not so good, huh? Help me keep my motivations golden.

Why do I do it? I hate it when I do things I know are wrong. You hate it, too, don't You? You hate the sin but love the sinner. . .me. I'm sooooo sorry I grieve Your big loving heart, Papa God. Your tears of forgiveness wipe away the messes I make over and over again.

Joy is a choice. It's always available and I can choose to be joyful, no matter what is happening around me. Help me choose joy. Amen.

May the challenges of life drive me to my knees.
Not in surrender. . .but in prayer.

Lord, how awesome it is to know that You think about me every minute of every day. Help me to faithfully set aside ten minutes a day to read Your love letters (the Bible) and think about You. You made me and gave me everything I have. It's the least I can do.

You told us many times in Your Word to respect our parents.
It must be important to You, so make it important to
me. . .whether I feel like it or not.

You created us girls as emotional beings, Lord. I'm glad about that most of the time. But sometimes I kind of, well, go crazy with my emotions. Help me learn self-control.

Like footprints in white beach sand,
help me leave joy-prints on everyone I meet!

When I'm sad, You truly are the
one who lifts my head (Psalm 3:3).

In Your Word, You said I should make my parents so glad I'm their daughter that they rejoice (Proverbs 23:24-26). Hmm. I may need to work a little harder on that one, Lord.

Thanks, gracious Father, for grace. It's amazing that You give good things to me when I don't deserve them. Grace—what an awesome feeling! It feels like getting 70 percent off when I thought an item was full price. You're the giver of all good things!

When trouble squeezes me like a toothpaste tube,
I pray that grace is what comes out!

"Anything is possible if a person believes."

Mark 9:23 NLT

Lord, help me take my eyes off myself and place them squarely on You. It's only then that I can give You all the praise and worship You deserve. Amen.

Creator of butterflies, humpback whales, june bugs, rainbows, waterfalls, and sunbeams, I worship You. Your fantastic array of creation takes my breath away.

Jesus, having You as my BFF is like
extra cheese on the pizza of life.

You transformed Mary, a poor teenager, into the honored mother of Jesus. Thank You, Father, for using girls like me to do great and mighty things for You.

God who makes the impossible possible,
I trust You with my life. Make a magnificent
butterfly emerge from this grungy cocoon. Amen.

I want to be a joyful person, Papa God. Joy spreads like spilled soda. People naturally want to hang around joyful people. Fizz me up with the kind of joy that lasts—Jesus-joy!

It makes me smile, Lord, to think You sent a message to a stubborn man named Balaam by a talking donkey (Numbers 22:21–33). Aren't donkeys supposed to be the stubborn ones? Ha! If You can use a donkey to do your work, You can surely use me!

Master Designer, help me remember
that I bear Your designer label.
I'm not fake Prada, I'm the real thing.

I think life is like driving a go-cart, Lord. I can't stay on the twisty, curvy track by myself, so I turn over the driver's seat to You. Now I sit back, let You do the steering, and enjoy the view.

Creator of flapping tongues, help me remember that a gentle answer calms down anger, but a harsh word only stirs it up big time (Proverbs 15:1). Sometimes I've just gotta put a muzzle on my mouth!

Forever is a looong time. I'm so happy I'll be spending it in heaven with You!

"For God so loved the world, that He gave His only begotten Son, that whoever believes in Him shall not perish, but have eternal life."
JOHN 3:16 NASB